THE OTHER COUNTRY

Also by Carol Ann Duffy

STANDING FEMALE NUDE
SELLING MANHATTAN
MEAN TIME
SELECTED POEMS

Anthologies

I WOULDN'T THANK YOU FOR A VALENTINE
ANVIL NEW POETS 2
STOPPING FOR DEATH

Carol Ann Duffy

THE OTHER COUNTRY

ANVIL PRESS POETRY

First published in 1990
by Anvil Press Poetry
Neptune House 70 Royal Hill London SE10 8RF

Reprinted 1991, 1993(twice)
New edition 1998

ISBN 0 85646 289 6

This book is published
with financial assistance from
The Arts Council of England

Set in Monotype Plantin Light by Anvil
Printed in Great Britain
at Morganprint (Blackheath) Ltd

A catalogue record for this book
is available from the British Library

ACKNOWLEDGEMENTS

Some of these poems have previously appeared in the
following publications: *Ambit, Bête Noire, Critical
Quarterly, First and Always* (Faber), *Foolscap, The
Guardian, Neighbours* (Peterloo), *The New Statesman, The
Orange Dove of Fiji* (Hutchinson), *Poetry Review, The
Rialto, Slow Dancer, Smoke, Soho Square* (Bloomsbury),
The Sunday Times, The Times Literary Supplement and
Vogue. Others have been broadcast on BBC Radio.

CONTENTS

Originally	7
In Mrs Tilscher's Class	8
Sit at Peace	9
Hometown	10
Translating the English, 1989	11
Mrs Skinner, North Street	12
Too Bad	13
Weasel Words	14
Poet for Our Times	15
Job Creation	16
Making Money	17
Talent Contest	19
Ape	20
The Legend	21
Descendants	22
We Remember Your Childhood Well	24
The Act of Imagination	25
Somewhere Someone's Eyes	27
Liar	28
Boy	29
Eley's Bullet	30
Following Francis	32
Survivor	33
An Afternoon with Rhiannon	34
Losers	35
M-M-Memory	36
Père Lachaise	37
Funeral	38
Dream of a Lost Friend	39
Like This	40
Who Loves You	41
Two Small Poems of Desire	42
Girlfriends	43
A Shilling for the Sea	44

Hard to Say   45
The Kissing Gate   46
Words, Wide Night   47
The *Darling* Letters   48
Away from Home   49
November   51
The Literature Act   52
River   53
The Way My Mother Speaks   54
In Your Mind   55

ORIGINALLY

We came from our own country in a red room
which fell through the fields, our mother singing
our father's name to the turn of the wheels.
My brothers cried, one of them bawling *Home,
Home*, as the miles rushed back to the city,
the street, the house, the vacant rooms
where we didn't live any more. I stared
at the eyes of a blind toy, holding its paw.

All childhood is an emigration. Some are slow,
leaving you standing, resigned, up an avenue
where no one you know stays. Others are sudden.
Your accent wrong. Corners, which seem familiar,
leading to unimagined, pebble-dashed estates, big boys
eating worms and shouting words you don't understand.
My parents' anxiety stirred like a loose tooth
in my head. *I want our own country*, I said.

But then you forget, or don't recall, or change,
and, seeing your brother swallow a slug, feel only
a skelf of shame. I remember my tongue
shedding its skin like a snake, my voice
in the classroom sounding just like the rest. Do I only think
I lost a river, culture, speech, sense of first space
and the right place? Now, *Where do you come from?*
strangers ask. *Originally?* And I hesitate.

IN MRS TILSCHER'S CLASS

You could travel up the Blue Nile
with your finger, tracing the route
while Mrs Tilscher chanted the scenery.
Tana. Ethiopia. Khartoum. Aswan.
That for an hour, then a skittle of milk
and the chalky Pyramids rubbed into dust.
A window opened with a long pole.
The laugh of a bell swung by a running child.

This was better than home. Enthralling books.
The classroom glowed like a sweet shop.
Sugar paper. Coloured shapes. Brady and Hindley
faded, like the faint, uneasy smudge of a mistake.
Mrs Tilscher loved you. Some mornings, you found
she'd left a good gold star by your name.
The scent of a pencil slowly, carefully, shaved.
A xylophone's nonsense heard from another form.

Over the Easter term, the inky tadpoles changed
from commas into exclamation marks. Three frogs
hopped in the playground, freed by a dunce,
followed by a line of kids, jumping and croaking
away from the lunch queue. A rough boy
told you how you were born. You kicked him, but stared
at your parents, appalled, when you got back home.

That feverish July, the air tasted of electricity.
A tangible alarm made you always untidy, hot,
fractious under the heavy, sexy sky. You asked her
how you were born and Mrs Tilscher smiled,
then turned away. Reports were handed out.
You ran through the gates, impatient to be grown,
as the sky split open into a thunderstorm.

SIT AT PEACE

When they gave you them to shell and you sat
on the back-doorstep, opening the small green envelopes
with your thumb, minding the queues of peas, you were
sitting at peace. *Sit at peace, sit at peace, all summer.*

When Muriel Purdy, embryonic cop, thwacked the back
of your knees with a bamboo-cane, mouth open, soundless
in a cave of pain, you ran to your house,
a greeting wain, to be kept in and told once again.

Nip was a dog. Fluff was a cat. They sat at peace
on a coloured-in mat, so why couldn't you? Sometimes
your questions were stray snipes over no-man's-land,
bringing sharp hands and the order you had to obey. *Sit –*

At – Peace! Jigsaws you couldn't do or dull stamps
you didn't want to collect arrived with the frost.
You would rather stand with your nose to the window, clouding
the strange blue view with your restless breath.

But the day you fell from the Parachute Tree, they came
from nowhere running, carried you in to a quiet room
you were glad of. A long still afternoon, dreamlike.
A voice saying *peace, sit at peace, sit at peace.*

HOMETOWN

for Jane and Alice Huntbach

In that town there was a different time,
a handful of years like old-fashioned sweets
you can't find anymore. I lived there.

What am I wearing as I pine for the future,
alone, down by the river by the Brine Baths
longing to get out? But I only threw a stone

at the face in the water and went home,
while behind me my features vanished,
trembled, reappeared, though I could not see.

Those streets, the gloomy shortcut by the church,
the triangle from school to home to the high field –
below which all roads sped away and led away –

and back again. Wherever I went then, I was
still there; fretting for something else, someone else,
somewhere else. Or else, I thought, I shall die.

And so I shall. Decades ahead of this, both of me,
then and now, pass each other like ghosts
in the empty market-place, where I imagine myself

to be older and away, or remember myself
younger, not loving this tuneless, flat bell
marking the time. Or moved to tears by its same sound.

TRANSLATING THE ENGLISH, 1989

'...and much of the poetry, alas, is lost in translation...'

Welcome to my country! We have here Edwina Currie
and The Sun newspaper. Much excitement.
Also the weather has been most improving
even in February. Daffodils. (Wordsworth. Up North.) If
    you like
Shakespeare or even Opera we have too the Black Market.
For two hundred quids we are talking Les Miserables,
nods being as good as winks. Don't eat the eggs.
Wheel-clamp. Dogs. Vagrants. A tour of our wonderful
capital city is not to be missed. The Fergie,
The Princess Di and the football hooligan, truly you will
like it here, Squire. Also we can be talking crack, smack
and Carling Black Label if we are so inclined. Don't
drink the H_2O. All very proud we now have
a green Prime Minister. What colour yours? Binbags.
You will be knowing of Charles Dickens and Terry Wogan
and Scotland. All this can be arranged for cash no questions.
Ireland not on. Fish and chips and the Official Secrets Act
second to none. Here we go. We are liking
a smashing good time like estate agents and Neighbours,
also Brookside for we are allowed four Channels.
How many you have? Last night of Proms. Andrew
Lloyd-Webber. Jeffrey Archer. Plenty culture you will be
    agreeing.
Also history and buildings. The Houses of Lords. Docklands.
Many thrills and high interest rates for own good. Muggers.
Much lead in petrol. Filth. Rule Britannia and child abuse.
Electronic tagging, Boss, ten pints and plenty rape. Queen
    Mum.
Channel Tunnel. You get here fast no problem to my country
my country my country welcome welcome welcome.

MRS SKINNER, NORTH STREET

Milk bottles. Light through net. No post. Cat,
come here by the window, settle down. Morning
in this street awakes unwashed; a stale wind
breathing litter, last night's godlessness. This place
is hellbound in a handcart, Cat, you mark
her words. Strumpet. Slut. A different man
for every child; a byword for disgrace.

Her dentures grin at her, gargling water
on the mantelpiece. The days are gone
for smiling, wearing them to chatter down the road.
Good morning. Morning. Lovely day. Over the years
she's suffered loss, bereavement, loneliness.
A terrace of strangers. An old ghost
mouthing curses behind a cloudy, nylon veil.

Scrounger. Workshy. Cat, where is the world
she married, was carried into up a scrubbed stone step?
The young louts roam the neighbourhood.
Breaking of glass. Chants. Sour abuse of aerosols.
That social worker called her *xenophobic*. When he left
she looked the word up. Fear, morbid dislike, of strangers.
Outside, the rain pours down relentlessly.

People scurry for shelter. How many hours
has she sat here, Cat, filled with bitterness
and knowing they'll none of them come?
Not till the day the smell is noticed.
Not till the day you're starving, Cat, and begin
to lick at the corpse. She twitches the curtain
as the Asian man next door runs through the rain.

TOO BAD

It was winter. Wilson had just said
we should have one in The Dog. So we did,
running through the blue wet streets
with our heads down, laughing, to get there,
down doubles in front of our drenched reflections.
The barmaid caught my eye in the mirror. Beautiful.

We had a job to do, but not till closing-time,
hard men knocking back the brandy, each of us
wearing revenge like a badge on his heart. Hatred
dresses in cheap anonymous suits, the kind
with an inside pocket for a small gun. *Good Health.*
I smiled at her. Warm rain, like blood, ran down my back.

I remembered my first time, my trembling hand
and Big Frank Connell hissing *Get a grip.*
Tonight, professional, I walked with the boys
along a filthy alley to the other pub, the one
where it happened, the one where the man
was putting on his coat, ready for home.

Home. Two weeks in a safe house and I'd be there,
glad of familiar accents and my dull wife.
He came out of a side door, clutching a carry-out.
Simple. Afterwards, Wilson was singing *dada da da*
Tom Someone, hang down your head and cry.
Too bad. I fancied that barmaid all right.

WEASEL WORDS

It was explained to Sir Robert Armstrong that
'weasel words' are 'words empty of meaning, like an
egg which has had its contents sucked out by a weasel'.

Let me repeat that we Weasels mean no harm.
You may have read that we are vicious hunters,
but this is absolutely not the case. Pure bias
on the part of your Natural History Book. *Hear, hear.*

We are long, slim-bodied carnivores with exceptionally
short legs and we have never denied this.
Furthermore, anyone here today could put a Weasel
down his trouser-leg and nothing would happen. *Weasel laughter.*

Which is more than can be said for the Ferrets opposite.
You can trust a Weasel, let me continue, a Weasel
does not break the spinal cord of its victim with one bite.
Weasel cheers. Our brown fur coats turn white in winter.

And as for eggs, here is a whole egg. It looks like an egg.
It is an egg. *Slurp.* An egg. *Slurp.* A whole egg. *Slurp... Slurp...*

POET FOR OUR TIMES

I write the headlines for a Daily Paper.
It's just a knack one's born with all-right-Squire.
You do not have to be an educator,
just bang the words down like they're screaming *Fire!*
CECIL-KEAYS ROW SHOCK TELLS EYETIE WAITER.
ENGLAND FAN CALLS WHINGEING FROG A LIAR.

Cheers. Thing is, you've got to grab attention
with just one phrase as punters rush on by.
I've made mistakes too numerous to mention,
so now we print the buggers inches high.
TOP MP PANTIE ROMP INCREASES TENSION.
RENT BOY: ROCK STAR PAID ME WELL TO LIE.

I like to think that I'm a sort of poet
for our times. My shout. Know what I mean?
I've got a special talent and I show it
in punchy haikus featuring the Queen.
DIPLOMAT IN BED WITH SERBO-CROAT.
EASTENDERS' BONKING SHOCK IS WELL-OBSCENE.

Of course, these days, there's not the sense of panic
you got a few years back. What with the box
et cet. I wish I'd been around when the Titanic
sank. To headline that, mate, would've been the tops.
SEE PAGE 3 TODAY GENTS THEY'RE GIGANTIC.
KINNOCK-BASHER MAGGIE PULLS OUT STOPS.

And, yes, I have a dream – make that a scotch, ta –
that kids will know my headlines off by heart.
IMMIGRANTS FLOOD IN CLAIMS HEATHROW WATCHER.
GREEN PARTY WOMAN IS A NIGHTCLUB TART.
The poems of the decade… *Stuff 'em! Gotcha!*
The instant tits and bottom line of art.

JOB CREATION

for Ian McMillan

They have shipped Gulliver up north.
He lies at the edge of the town,
sleeping.
His snores are thunder in the night.

Round here, we reckon they have drugged him
or we dream he is a landscape
which might drag itself up and walk.

Here are ropes, they said.
Tie him down.
We will pay you.
Tie Gulliver down with these ropes.

I slaved all day at his left knee,
until the sun went down
behind it
and clouds gathered on his eyes

and darkness settled on his shoulders
like a job.

MAKING MONEY

Turnover. Profit. Readies. Cash. Loot. Dough. Income. Stash.
Dosh. Bread. Finance. Brass. I give my tongue over
to money; the taste of warm rust in a chipped mug
of tap-water. Drink some yourself. Consider
an Indian man in Delhi, Salaamat the *niyariwallah*,
who squats by an open drain for hours, sifting shit
for the price of a chapati. More than that. His hands
in crumbling gloves of crap pray at the drains
for the pearls in slime his grandfather swore he found.

Megabucks. Wages. Interest. Wealth. I sniff and snuffle
for a whiff of pelf; the stench of an abattoir blown
by a stale wind over the fields. Roll up a fiver,
snort. Meet Kim. Kim will give you the works,
her own worst enema, suck you, lick you, squeal
red weals to your whip, be nun, nurse, nanny,
nymph on a credit card. Don't worry.
Kim's only in it for the money. Lucre. Tin. Dibs.

I put my ear to brass lips; a small fire's whisper
close to a forest. Listen. His cellular telephone
rings in the Bull's car. Golden hello. Big deal. Now get this
straight. *Making a living is making a killing these days.*
Jobbers and brokers buzz. He paints out a landscape
by number. The Bull. Seriously rich. Nasty. One of us.

Salary. Boodle. Oof. Blunt. Shekels. Lolly. Gelt. Funds.
I wallow in coin, naked; the scary caress of a fake hand
on my flesh. Get stuck in. Bergama. The boys from the bazaar
hide on the target-range, watching the soldiers fire. Between
    bursts,
they rush for the spent shells, cart them away for scrap.
Here is the catch. Some shells don't explode. Ahmat
runs over grass, lucky for six months, so far. So
bomb-collectors die young. But the money's good.

Palmgrease. Smackers. Greenbacks. Wads. I widen my eyes
at a fortune; a set of knives on black cloth, shining,
utterly beautiful. Weep. The economy booms
like cannon, far out at sea on a lone ship. We leave
our places of work, tired, in the shortening hours, in the time
of night our town could be anywhere, and some of us pause
in the square, where a clown makes money swallowing fire.

TALENT CONTEST

At the end of the pier, an open-air theatre, a crowd
who have paid to come in, wooden slats, the sea slopping out
like beer in a cracked plastic cup, one scrunched cloud
like a boarding-house towel, grey. You're a contestant.

Take my advice, leave now. Head for the Gaiety Bar
or the rifle-range. Better still, slink to a seat, knot your
    handkerchief
over your head and watch. The spoon-player has no chance.
Farmyard Noises takes out his teeth. Ambitious. In for the lot.

Why do you sneer? A cheap song sung badly
pleases the crowd. The tap-dancer spreads out his arms
and grins, a man tortured. Beware the ventriloquist,
the dark horse, whose thrown voice juggles the truth.

You don't want to hear this. Poweran moneyan fame you say
    to yourself
like a blessing, then you're into the act. Make 'em laugh. A
    seagull
shrieks at you out of the blue. Make 'em cry. A baby
sobs and sobs in a pram at the end of a row.

Applause. A show of hands from plonkers with day-jobs.
    Cheers.
You're kind to the yodeller later, sneaky and modest, not
    letting on
you thought it a piece of piss. Talent. A doubt like faraway
    thunder
threatens to ruin the day, that it's squandered on this.

APE

There is a male silverback on the calendar.
Behind him the jungle is defocused,
except in one corner, where trees gargle the sun.

After you have numbered the days, you tear off
the page. His eyes hold your eyes
as you crumple a forest in your fist.

THE LEGEND

Some say it was seven tons of meat in a thick black hide
you could build a boat from, stayed close to the river
on the flipside of the sun where the giant forests were.

Had shy, old eyes. You'd need both those hands for one.
Maybe. Walked in placid herds under a jungly, sweating roof
just breathing; a dry electric wind you could hear a mile off.

Huge feet. Some say if it rained you could fish in a footprint,
fruit fell when it passed. It moved, food happened, simple.
You think of a warm, inky cave and you got its mouth all right.

You dream up a yard of sandpaper, damp, you're talking
    tongue.
Eat? Its own weight in a week. And water. Some say
the sweat steamed from its back in small grey clouds.

But big. Enormous. Spine like the mast on a galleon.
Ears like sails gasping for a wind. You picture
a rope you could hang a man from, you're seeing its tail.

Tusks like bannisters. I almost believe myself. Can you
drum up a roar as wide as a continent, a deep hot note
that bellowed out and belonged to the melting air? You got it.

But people have always lied! You know some say it had a trunk
like a soft telescope, that it looked up along it at the sky
and balanced a bright, gone star on the end, and it died.

DESCENDANTS

Most of us worked the Lancashire vineyards all year and a few
                                        freak redheads died.
We were well-nuked. Knackered. The gaffers gave us
                                        a bonus
in Burgdy and Claray. Big fucking deal, we thought, we'd been
                                        robbing them blind
for months. Drink enough of it, you can juggle with snakes,
                                        no sweat.

Some nights, me and Sarah went down to the ocean
                                        with a few flasks
and a groundsheet and we'd have it off three or four times
                                        in a night
that barely got dark. For hours, you could hear the dolphins
                                        rearing up
as if they were after something. Strange bastards. I like
                                        dolphins.

Anyway. She's soft, Sarah. She can read. Big green moon
                                        and her with a book
of *poetry* her Gran had. Nuke me. Nice words, right enough,
                                        and I love the girl,
but I'd had plenty. *Winter*, I goes, *Spring, Autumn, Summer,*
                                        don't give me
that crap, Sarah, and I flung the book over the white sand,
                                        into the waves,

beyond the dolphins. Click-click. Sad. I hate the
                                        bastard past, see,
I'd piss on an ancestor as soon as trace one. *What*
                                        fucking seasons

I says to her, just look at us now. So we looked.
                              At each other.
At the trembling unsafe sky. And she started, didn't she,
                                        to cry.
Tears over her lovely blotchy purple face. It got to me.

WE REMEMBER YOUR
CHILDHOOD WELL

Nobody hurt you. Nobody turned off the light and argued
with somebody else all night. The bad man on the moors
was only a movie you saw. Nobody locked the door.

Your questions were answered fully. No. That didn't occur.
You couldn't sing anyway, cared less. The moment's a blur, a
    Film Fun
laughing itself to death in the coal fire. Anyone's guess.

Nobody forced you. You wanted to go that day. Begged. You
    chose
the dress. Here are the pictures, look at you. Look at us all,
smiling and waving, younger. The whole thing is inside your
    head.

What you recall are impressions; we have the facts. We called
    the tune.
The secret police of your childhood were older and wiser than
    you, bigger
than you. Call back the sound of their voices. Boom. Boom.
    Boom.

Nobody sent you away. That was an extra holiday, with people
you seemed to like. They were firm, there was nothing to fear.
There was none but yourself to blame if it ended in tears.

What does it matter now? No, no, nobody left the skidmarks
    of sin
on your soul and laid you wide open for Hell. You were loved.
Always. We did what was best. We remember your childhood
    well.

THE ACT OF IMAGINATION

Under the Act, the following things may be
prosecuted for appalling the Imagination.

Ten More Years.
A dog playing Beethoven's 'Moonlight Sonata'.
President Quayle.

The pyjamas of Tax Inspectors.
The Beef Tapeworm (*Taenia Saginata*).
British Rail.

Picking someone else's nose.
The Repatriation Charter.
Gaol.

The men. The Crucifix. The nails.

The sound of the neighbours having sex.
The Hanging Lobby.
The Bomb.

Glow-in-the-dark Durex.
A Hubby.
Bedtime with Nancy and Ron.

The sweet smell of success.
A camel's jobby.
On

and on. And on. And on.

Eating the weakest survivor.
A small hard lump.
Drinking meths.

Going as Lady Godiva.
A parachute jump.
One breast.

Homeless and down to a fiver.
A hump.
Bad breath.

Here is a space to fill in things you suggest.

Death.

SOMEWHERE SOMEONE'S EYES

What if there had been a painter – he was drunk – *equal
to Picasso, who filled his canvases for years,
destroyed them all, and died?* It was the old one
about the tree, the empty wood, the unheard moan
of a great oak falling unobserved. We thought
we'd humour him. *Or a composer, whose scores
were never played – who also died – nor ever found?*

Because I remember this, a cool room flares
with the heat of a winter's fire, briefly. His face
glowed red-brown when he spoke to the flames.
I recollect it more than well, smell malt. *What
happens to the lost?* The shadow his mind made legless
lurched against the wall, glass raised. He cursed,
demanded an answer from the dog. All night it snowed.

Somewhere… he said, but we'd had enough, began
to joke and get half-screwed ourselves. *Somewhere someone's …*
Outside, the trees shifted under their soft burdens,
or I imagine so. Our footsteps disappeared. It was easy
to laugh in that snug house, talk nonsense
half the night, drink. Across the white fields somewhere
someone's eyes blazed as they burned words in their mouth.

LIAR

She made things up: for example, that she was really
a man. After she'd taken off her cotton floral
day-frock she was him alright, in her head,
dressed in that heavy herringbone from Oxfam.
He was called Susan actually. The eyes in the mirror
knew that, but she could stare them out.

Of course, a job; of course, a humdrum city flat;
of course, the usual friends. Lover? Sometimes.
She lived like you do, a dozen slack rope-ends
in each dream hand, tugging uselessly on memory
or hope. Frayed. She told stories. *I lived
in Moscow once... I nearly drowned...* Rotten.

Lightning struck me and I'm here to tell... Liar.
Hyperbole, falsehood, fiction, fib were pebbles tossed
at the evening's flat pool; her bright eyes
fixed on the ripples. No one believed her.
Our secret films are private affairs, watched
behind the eyes. She spoke in subtitles. Not on.

From bad to worse. The ambulance whinged all the way
to the park where she played with the stolen child.
You know the rest. The man in the long white wig
who found her sadly confused. The top psychiatrist
who studied her in gaol, then went back home and did
what he does every night to the Princess of Wales.

BOY

I liked being small. When I'm on my own
I'm small. I put my pyjamas on
and hum to myself. I like doing that.

What I don't like is being large, you know,
grown-up. Just like that. Whoosh. Hairy.
I think of myself as a boy. Safe slippers.

The world is terror. Small you can go *As I*
lay down my head to sleep, I pray... I remember
my three wishes sucked up a chimney of flame.

I can do it though. There was an older woman
who gave me a bath. She was joking, of course,
but I wasn't. I said *Mummy* to her. Off-guard.

Now it's a question of getting the wording right
for the Lonely Hearts verse. There must be someone
out there who's kind to boys. Even if they grew.

ELEY'S BULLET

Out walking in the fields, Eley found a bullet
with his name on it. Pheasants *korred*
and whirred at the sound of gunfire.
Eley's dog began to whine. England
was turning brown at the edges. Autumn. Rime
in the air. A cool bullet in his palm.

Eley went home. He put the tiny missile
in a matchbox and put that next to a pistol
in the drawer of his old desk. His dog
sat at his feet by the coal fire as he drank
a large whisky, then another one, but this
was usual. Eley went up the stairs to his bath.

He was in love with a woman in the town. The water
was just right, slid over his skin as he gave out
a long low satisfied moan into the steam.
His telephone began to ring and Eley cursed,
then dripped along the hall. She was in a call-box.
She'd lied all afternoon and tonight she was free.

The woman was married. Eley laughed aloud
with apprehension and delight, the world
expanded as he thought of her, his dog
trembled under his hand. Eley knelt,
he hugged the dog till it barked. Outside, the wind
knew something was on and nudged at the clouds.

They lay in each other's arms, as if what they had done
together had broken the pair of them. The woman
was half-asleep and Eley was telling himself
how he would spend a wish, if he could have only one
for the whole of his life. His fingers counted
the beads of her back as he talked in the dark.

At ten, Eley came into the bedroom with drinks.
She was combing her hair at the mirror. His eyes
seemed to hurt at the sight. She told him sorry,
but this was the last time. She tried to smile.
He stared, then said her words himself, the way
he'd spoken Latin as a boy. Dead language.

By midnight the moon was over the house, full
and lethal, and Eley alone. He went to his desk
with a bottle and started to write. Upstairs,
the dog sniffed at the tepid bed. Eley held
his head in his hands and wanted to cry,
but *Beloved* he wrote and *forever* and *why*.

Some men have no luck. Eley knew he'd as well
send her his ear as mail these stale words,
although he could taste her still. Nearby, a bullet
was there for the right moment and the right man.
He got out his gun, slowly, not even thinking,
and loaded it. Now he would choose. He paused.

He could finish the booze, sleep without dreams
with the morning to face, the loss of her
sore as the sunlight; or open his mouth
for a gun with his name on its bullet to roar
in his brains. Thunder or silence. Eley wished to God
he'd never loved. And then the frightened whimper of a dog.

FOLLOWING FRANCIS

Watch me. I start with a low whistle, twist it,
pitch it higher and thinner till the kestrel treads air.
There! I have a genius for this, which I offer
to God. Do they say I am crazy, brother?

Yes, they say that. My own wife said it. *Dropping everything*
and following that fool! You want to be covered
in birdshit? You make me sick. I left anyway,
hurried to the woods to meet him. Francis. Francis.
We had nothing. Later, I wept in his arms like a boy;
his hands were a woman's, plucking my tears off, tasting them.

We are animals, he said.

I am more practical. He fumbles with two sticks
hoping for fire; swears, laughs, cups glow-worms
in his palm while I start up a flame. Some nights
we've company, local accents in the dusk. He sees
my jealousy flare beneath dark trees. He knows.
I know he knows. When he looks at me, he thinks

I cannot tame this.

This evening, Francis preaches to the birds. If he is crazy,
what does that make me? I close my eyes. Tell my children
we move north tomorrow, away from here where the world
sings through cool grass, water, air, a saint's voice.
Tell them that what I am doing I do from choice.

He holds a fist to the sky and a hawk swoops down.

SURVIVOR

For some time now, at the curve of my mind,
I have longed to embrace my brother, my sister, myself,
when we were seven years old. It is making me ill.

Also my first love, who was fifteen, Leeds, I know
it is thirty years, but when I remember him now
I can feel his wet, young face in my hands, melting
snow, my empty hands. This is bereavement.

Or I spend the weekend in bed, dozing, lounging
in the past. Why has this happened? I mime
the gone years where I lived. I want them back.

My lover rises and plunges above me, not knowing
I have hidden myself in my heart, where I rock
and weep for what has been stolen, lost. Please.
It is like an earthquake and no one to tell.

AN AFTERNOON WITH RHIANNON

The night before, our host had pointed out the Building
Larkin feared. *He was right*, I said, suddenly cold
and wanting home; cold later, too, in bed, listening
to wind and rain whip in to the lonely, misplaced town.

But lunchtime brought a clip of spring; a gold man mounted
on a prancing golden horse en route to the pier-head
    rendezvous
where your mother set you down. We watched you bumble
after pigeons, squeal as sun and air and Humber spun you
    around.

Around and around. Then you shouted *Boat!*, pointing
at nothing, *Boat!*, an empty river, a boatless blue painting
you haven't begun yet. A small child's daylight
is a safer place than a poet's slow, appalling, ticking night;

a place where you say, in a voice so new it shines, *I like
buildings!* The older people look, the shy town smiles.

LOSERS

Con-artists, barefaced liars, clocks shuffle the hours slowly.
Remember the hands you were dealt, the full-house of love,
the ace-high you bluffed on. Never again. Each day
is a new game, sucker, with mornings and midnights
raked in by the dealer. Did you think you could keep those
    cards?

Imagination is memory. We are the fools who dwell in time
outside of time. One saves up for a lifelong dream, another
spends all she has on a summer decades ago. The clocks
click like chips in a casino, piled to a wobbly tower. An hour
fills up with rain. An hour runs down a gutter into a drain.

Where do you live? In a kiss in a darkened cricket pavilion
after the war? Banker? In the scent, from nowhere, of apples
seconds before she arrived? Poet? You don't live here
and now. Where? In the day your mother didn't come home?
    Priest?
In the chalky air of the classroom, still? Doctor? Assassin?
    Whore?

Look at the time. There will be more but there is always less.
Place your bets. Mostly we do not notice our latest loss
under the rigged clocks. Remember the night we won! The
    times
it hurts are when we grab the moment for ourselves, nearly –
the corniest sunset, taste of a lover's tears, a fistful of snow –

and the bankrupt feeling we have as it disappears.

M-M-MEMORY

Scooping spilt, soft, broken oil
with a silver spoon
from a flagstone floor
into a clay bowl –

the dull scrape of the spoon
on the cool stone,
lukewarm drops in the bowl –

m-m-memory.

Kneel there,
words like fossils
trapped in the roof of the mouth,
forgotten, half-forgotten, half-
recalled, the tongue dreaming
it can trace their shape.

Names, ghosts, m-memory.

Through the high window of the hall
clouds obfuscate the sun
and you sit, exhaling grey smoke
into a purpling, religious light
trying to remember everything

perfectly
in time and space
where you cannot.

Those unstrung beads of oil
seem precious now, now
that the light has changed.

PÈRE LACHAISE

for Monty Cohen

Along the ruined avenues the long gone lie
under the old stones. For 10 francs, a map unravels
the crumbling paths which lead to the late great.
A silent town. A vast, perplexing pause.

The living come, murmuring with fresh flowers, their maps
fluttering like white flags in the slight breeze.
April. Beginning of spring. Lilies for Oscar,
one red rose for Colette. Remembrance. Do not forget.

Turn left for Seurat, Chopin, Proust, and Gertrude Stein
with nothing more to say. Below the breathing trees
a thousand lost talents dream into dust; decay
into largely familiar names for a stranger's bouquet.

Forever dead. Say these words and let their meaning
dizzy you like the scent of innumerable petals
here in Père Lachaise. The sad tourists stand
by the graves, reciting the titles of poems, paintings, songs,

things which have brought them here for the afternoon.
We thread our way through the cemetery, misquoting
or humming quietly and almost comforted.
Two young men embrace near Piaf's tomb.

FUNERAL

Say milky cocoa we'd say,
you had the accent for it,
drunk you sometimes would. *Milky*

cocoa. Preston. We'd all
laugh. *Milky cocoa*. Drunk,
drunk. You laughed, saying it.

From all over the city
mourners swarmed, a demo against
death, into the cemetery.

You asked for nothing.
Three gravediggers, two minutes
of silence in the wind. Black

cars took us back. Serious
drinking. Awkward ghosts
getting the ale in. All afternoon

we said your name, repeated
the prayers of anecdotes,
bereaved and drunk

enough to think you might arrive,
say milky cocoa... Milky
cocoa, until we knew you'd gone.

DREAM OF A LOST FRIEND

You were dead, but we met, dreaming,
before you had died. Your name, twice,
then you turned, pale, unwell. *My dear,*
my dear, must this be? A public building
where I've never been, and, on the wall,
an AIDS poster. Your white lips. *Help me.*

We embraced, standing in a long corridor
which harboured a fierce pain neither of us felt yet.
The words you spoke were frenzied prayers
to Chemistry; or you laughed, a child-man's laugh,
innocent, hysterical, out of your skull. *It's only*
a dream, I heard myself saying, *only a bad dream.*

Some of our best friends nurture a virus, an idle,
charmed, purposeful enemy, and it dreams
they are dead already. In fashionable restaurants,
over the crudités, the healthy imagine a time
when all these careful moments will be dreamed
and dreamed again. *You look well. How do you feel?*

Then, as I slept, you backed away from me, crying
and offering a series of dates for lunch, waving.
I missed your funeral, I said, knowing you couldn't hear
at the end of the corridor, thumbs up, acting.
Where there's life… Awake, alive, for months I think of you
almost hopeful in a bad dream where you were long dead.

LIKE THIS

When you die in the city where everyone was young,
at the end of the dark, drunken years that kept you there,
old friends walk up through the wild streets
to the alehouse, whose watery, yellow lights
are a faint, hopeless beacon in the night,
and, nearer now to you, they get in the rounds,
the solemn, slow, ceremonial rounds which soften their tongues
to speak brief epitaphs of love, regret; meanwhile,
you lie in an ice-cold drawer, two postal codes away,
without recall or recourse, although you had both,
although you are not yet old, although a woman is crying
in the big house on the park where they carried you out
for the last time, where you were told how it would end,
how it would be like this unless, unless. And it is.

WHO LOVES YOU

I worry about you travelling in those mystical machines.
Every day people fall from the clouds, dead.
Breathe in and out and in and out easy.
Safety, safely, safe home.

Your photograph is in the fridge, smiles when the light comes on.
All the time people are burnt in the public places.
Rest where the cool trees drop to a gentle shade.
Safety, safely, safe home.

Don't lie down on the sands where the hole in the sky is.
Too many people being gnawed to shreds.
Send me your voice however it comes across oceans.
Safety, safely, safe home.

The loveless men and homeless boys are out there and angry.
Nightly people end their lives in the shortcut.
Walk in the light, steadily hurry towards me.
Safety, safely, safe home. (Who loves you?)
Safety, safely, safe home.

TWO SMALL POEMS OF DESIRE

I

The little sounds I make against your skin
don't mean anything. They make me
an animal learning vowels; not that I know
I do this, but I hear them
floating away over your shoulders, sticking
to the ceiling. *Aa Ee Iy Oh Uu.*

Are they sounds of surprise
at the strange ghosts your nakedness makes
moving above me in how much light
a net can catch?

Who cares. Sometimes language virtuously used
is language badly used. It's tough
and difficult and true to say
I love you when you do these things to me.

2

The way I prefer to play you back
is naked in the cool lawn of those green sheets,
just afterwards,
and saying *What secret am I?*

I am brought up sharp in a busy street,
staring inwards as you put down your drink
and touch me again. *How does it feel?*

It feels like tiny gardens
growing in the palms of the hands,
invisible,
sweet, if they had a scent.

GIRLFRIENDS

derived from Verlaine
for John Griffith

That hot September night, we slept in a single bed,
naked, and on our frail bodies the sweat
cooled and renewed itself. I reached out my arms
and you, hands on my breasts, kissed me. Evening of amber.

Our nightgowns lay on the floor where you fell to your knees
and became ferocious, pressed your head to my stomach,
your mouth to the red gold, the pink shadows; except
I did not see it like this at the time, but arched

my back and squeezed water from the sultry air
with my fists. Also I remember hearing, clearly
but distantly, a siren some streets away – *de*

da de da de da – which mingled with my own
absurd cries, so that I looked up, even then,
to see my fingers counting themselves, dancing.

A SHILLING FOR THE SEA

You get a shilling if you see it first.
You take your lover to a bar nearby, late evening,
spend it all night and still have change. If,

if it were me, if it were you, we'd drink up
and leave; screw on the beach, with my bare arse
soaked by the night-tide's waves, your face moving
between mine and that gambler's throw of stars.

Then we'd dress and go back to the bar, order
the same again, and who's this whispering filthy suggestions
into my ear? *My tongue in the sea slow salt wet ...*

Yes. All for a shilling, if you play that game.

HARD TO SAY

I asked him to give me an image for Love, something I could see,
or imagine seeing, or something that, because of the word
for its smell, would make me remember, something possible
to hear. *Don't just say love,* I said, *love, love, I love you.*

On the way home, I thought of our love and how, lately,
I too have grown lazy in expressing it, snuggling up to you
in bed, idly murmuring those tired clichés without even thinking.
My words have been grubby confetti, faded, tacky, blown far

from the wedding feast. And so it was, with a sudden shock of
      love,
like a peacock flashing wide its hundred eyes, or a boy's voice
flinging top G to the roof of an empty church, or a bottle
of French perfume knocked off the shelf, spilling into the steamy
      bath,

I wanted you. After the wine, the flowers I brought you drowned
in the darkening light. As we slept, we breathed their scent all
      night.

THE KISSING GATE

After I've spoken to you, I walk out to the gate
at the edge of the field, watch a bird make a nonsense
of the air, and wish. This is not my landscape,
though I feel at home here, in a way, in a light
that rolls a dreg of memory around itself, spills it.
You'll not see it now. The bird. Me at the gate. Call it
a yellowy light. There it goes, into the grass, green,

greener, going. Love holds words to itself, repeats them
till they're smooth, sit silent on the tongue
like a small stone you sucked once, for some reason,
on a beach. I tell myself the things you'd like to do to me
if you were here, where there's no one to see for miles,
where I sense myself grow lighter and heavier, dizzy, solid,
and a bird swoops down, down, the light follows it.

WORDS, WIDE NIGHT

Somewhere on the other side of this wide night
and the distance between us, I am thinking of you.
The room is turning slowly away from the moon.

This is pleasurable. Or shall I cross that out and say
it is sad? In one of the tenses I singing
an impossible song of desire that you cannot hear.

La lala la. See? I close my eyes and imagine
the dark hills I would have to cross
to reach you. For I am in love with you and this

is what it is like or what it is like in words.

THE DARLING LETTERS

Some keep them in shoeboxes away from the light,
sore memories blinking out as the lid lifts,
their own recklessness written all over them. *My own …*
Private jokes, no longer comprehended, pull their punchlines,
fall flat in the gaps between endearments. *What
are you wearing?*

> *Don't ever change.*

They start with *Darling*; end in recriminations,
absence, sense of loss. Even now, the fist's bud flowers
into trembling, the fingers trace each line and see
the future then. *Always…* Nobody burns them,
the *Darling* letters, stiff in their cardboard coffins.

Babykins… We all had strange names
which make us blush, as though we'd murdered
someone under an alias, long ago. *I'll die
without you.* Die. Once in a while, alone,
we take them out to read again, the heart thudding
like a spade on buried bones.